THE EGO DRIVEN LIFE

A CASE OF MISTAKEN IDENTITY........

BY RUSSELL WINGOOD

This book is dedicated to those humans who toil collectively under the mistaken illusion that who they are actually who they are pretending to be.

The human ego creates a myriad of experiences and is a most interesting subject, for every human has one; there is no one who is immune. For the most part many people are unaware of its presence much less its power. At this particular moment in history the human ego has become very troubling both individually and collectively. The ego is most difficult to explain and investigate because it is the very foundation and basis of who we are in one sense, but in another entirely different sense it is everything that we are not. I have chosen in this book of meditations on the ego to delve into both aspects of the self, the lower or ego based self and the higher or spiritual self and hopefully be able to bring to light both the illusion and the mistaken identity that we call our ego.

*T*he more that we contemplate our ego; the more power that we give it.

★

*T*he human ego is not as frail and helpless as it would like us to believe.

*W*e energize the ego through conflict and drama, inflating it with words and actions all at the expense of our peace and well being.

*T*he ego loves to make promises that it has no intention of keeping.

*T*he ego likes to make us feel special and different when in fact the ego is a self created image that we have of ourselves that has no more reality than a cloud passing overhead.

*T*he ego loves to make the ordinary person feel quite extraordinary.

---

*T*he sooner that one realizes their ego to be a liability in most cases the happier they will be in the long run.

★

*T*he same perfection that our ego demands in others is never seen as being needed ourself.

---

*H*ow can one be truly loving when we are a slave to our lower self or ego?

*I*n the pure universal consciousness of the universe there was never a separate "I" only the illusion of an "I" which was created by the Ego.

*T*he greater understanding man has of his true place in the universe the less he will have to rely on and depend on his ego.

★

*A*lmost all profound spiritual crises' come from a radical misidentification with the ego at the expense of ones divine higher self.

The ego creates an illusion of separateness to not only inflate itself but also to convince us of it necessity.

★

The true understanding of the ego may very well come from the ego itself.

*A*ll radical spiritual transformation has its genesis in the thinning out and awareness of ones ego.

*S*tubbornness is a trait of the ego that keeps us locked into the belief that we are the individual doers of all of our deeds.

*T*he games that we play with others are nothing compared to the games that our ego plays on us.

*T*rue generosity of spirit can only take place in the absence of the ego.

*T*he human organism has created an image of itself called the ego to give itself a personality upon which to exist in the human world.

★

*T*he source of our suffering originates not in our self but in our ego.

*A*ll conflicts emanate from and flow back to the ego.

*T*he ego can only have as much power as we choose to give it through our unconsciousness.

*T*he wisdom that the ego has for us is hidden in our higher self.

★

*T*he most radical change that we can make in ourselves is a direct awareness of ones ego.

*T*he ego creates the unfulfilled desires that cause the tension and unhappiness in human beings.

*I*f we were able to see how much of our higher self that the ego hid from us we would be both baffled and amazed.

*T*he ego picks and chooses the people that it wants for us to be with, but is they in the end that the higher self would have chosen?

*T*he ego plays dual roles; it is both the attention getter and also the thing that needs to be the center of attention.

*T*he ego pursues its own agenda often to the exclusion of all common sense.

*T*he critical nature of the ego is a mechanical response to a condition that the ego does not approve of.

*W*hen a person is in love with their opinions what they are actually in love with is their ego.

★

*T*o identify with ones ego as the center of ones whole being is to live a life so diminished that it hardly qualifies as living.

*T*he ego sees two where there is and always was only one.

*T*rust and faith in God thins out and weakens the ego so that we can become one with our higher self.

The truth of life hidden by the ego seems no more real than a mirage.

★

The ego is like a shadow that follows around but is simply an illusion caused by the sun.

*W*hen the ego dies we then are reborn in the spirit of our true and higher self.

★

*G*od purifies each soul in its own way, in its own time and in accordance with its needs.

*W*hy does the ego always want to remodel another's house when its own is need of a major remodel?

*A*ll conceptualization begins with an ignorance of our true self and a blind allegiance to the ego.

Mans egoistic personality is that mechanical part of ourselves that keeps us from seeing the divine in both ourselves and others.

We are mostly slaves to the ego whether we want to believe it or not.

*T*he ego is the grand instigator, the master of unresolved conflict.

⭐

*F*reedom from our lower self can only come about when are liberated from the ego.

*O*ur ego tells us what we want to hear, most often to the detriment of our true higher self.

★

*H*ow many times one must be pushed, pulled and disillusioned by the ego before we begin to see its folly.

*T*he ego loves to create a veil of separation between ourselves and others as we are much easier to conquer when we are divided.

*G*ossip creates an environment for the human ego that both nourishes it and perpetuates it.

*T*he human ego in a sense is a weapon; if it is not moderated and used properly it can cause a great deal of destruction.

*T*he thinned out or weakened ego provides the best foundation for dynamic spiritual growth.

*O*ur ego derives it's consciousness from our unconsciousness.

★

*T*he reality of the ego is actually no greater than that of our shadow on a sunny day.

*W*hen we are able to see life from totality we can only laugh at the various permutations that our ego has put us through.

*T*he importance that one places on ones self is flawed in many respects, the greatest reason being that the ego was the creator of that importance.

*T*he ego's favorite word is "more" while the spirits is "less."

★

*O*ur ego greatly exaggerates many of life's dilemmas so as to provide us with an illusory safety blanket in our times of most dire necessity.

The stubbornness of the full blown egoistic personality is quite a sight to behold.

The ego is suspicious of anything that tries to make a change in its illusory comfort ability.

The foolish and silly games of the ego need us to be willing participants or the game cannot be played.

★

Our ego is often very successful at making us feel and seen smaller than we actually are.

*T*o make major changes in ones egoistic personality requires radical determination and rigorous discernment.

*W*hen we begin understand how the ego works in ourselves we can then see how it works in others.

*M*ans addiction to his ego is both his folly and one day his ultimate salvation.

*T*he salvation that man seeks is right here right now although the ego tells us that it is impractical and unnecessary to begin that search today.

The ability of our ego to keep us under its spell is based largely on the mistaken opinion that we cannot survive or exist without it.

★

The ego preens prances and struts its stuff...for the benefit of whom?

*M*an's created ego by divine hypnosis is one of nature's most miraculous illusions.

★

*T*he fear of the unknown is what keeps the common man, attached in many cases quite spectacularly, to his very ordinary ego.

*S*ooner or later in whatever lifetime it happens we will have to come face to face with our ego for the purpose of self realization of our true and divine higher self.

*T*he games and drama of man's individual ego are quite often necessary elements for the cosmic play of life to unfold and evolution to take place.

*T*he egoic personality of man is the veil which distracts and hides from him his true divine inheritance.

*T*he ego is that thing that tells you that your life is absolutely perfect when you know darn well that it is not.

*T*he underlying spirit of the universal self provides the safe and secure backdrop for those who want to transition away from the egoic personality

*C*an you imagine the surprise of the ego when for so long it had the rule of the roost and now its very existence gets threatened.

*T*he ego is such a master of deceit and deception that it can convince a person that it is better to hate than it is to love and forgive.

*T*he egos supreme folly is in its belief that Man may never wake up to the power and realization of the one Universal self.

*T*he illusion that we call living is given its reality by the egoic personality which in and of itself is an illusion.

*O*ne must eventually come to a realization of the folly of ones ego to enter the kingdom of heaven.

*T*he illusion that we are a separate entity all alone in the Cosmos is a creation of the ego to ensure its existence.

*O*ne of the egos greatest deceptions is its ability to get us to continue to believe and follow it when all intuition points to doing just the opposite.

*T*he is a higher state of consciousness available to all that is egoless and where "so called" miracles are commonplace.

*I*n actuality all creations of the universe are egoless; however by virtue of our own egos we view everything else as having an ego.

*T*he illusory life lived primarily through the egoic personality is a lie.

★

*A*lthough in our human existence there was never really two of anything, our ego has created a myriad of images that have caused us to see separation when there never really was any.

A strong ego is thought to be necessary as a survival technique but in actuality that survival was an illusion created by the ego for the ego.

*A*ny thoughts or actions that we think that we do individually are simply illusions created by the ego to sustain its existence.

A radical awareness of ones ego is necessary for the radical transformation of it.

*T*he death of the dream of the ego can only be finalized through the grace of God's will.

*M*any humans enjoy the company of their ego and simply have no desire to change anything about themselves.

*A*t this stage in mankind's evolution the ego is playing a predominate part in the role of life as opposed to seemingly forgotten or misunderstood spirit of our divine higher self.

*M*any forms of neurosis and depression are simply due in fact to a metaphysical disconnection in the individual, the covering up of ones true identity by its fictitious opposite, the ego.

★

*G*od is most always hard to see with the ever present ego in the way.

*M*ans love affair with his ego is his greatest cause of discontent and anxiety.

★

*T*rue compassion and kindness are very rare and most always involve the ulterior motives of ones ego.

*T*hose who leave life's major decisions to their ego must one day pay the consequences for that choice.

*M*ans love for his fellow man only extends as far as his ego will let him.

The deconstruction of ones ego requires great courage but more importantly great patience.

★

The strength of the ego lies in its power of persuasion.

*S*elf pride convinces us that our ego knows more than it does.

★

*T*he egoic human personality is very mechanical in response to another's words and actions.

*H*uman beings have almost a compulsive egoic need to convince others that their way is the right way and that their opinion is the correct one.

*T*rue freedom from ones ego must begin with the realization that although the ego has been your identity for your whole life it has been a case of mistaken identity and that ones true and higher self is just a change in consciousness away.

*T*he ego craves the materialistic lifestyle as a way to keep our focus on external things rather than internally on our true and divine higher self.

*T*he ego dislikes the truth for it shines the light of our pure being upon our deceptive lower self.

*W*hen we become conscious and aware of our actions the ego has less room to operate.

★

*T*he greatest fallacy of man lies in his belief that he is separate from all others and that he is the individual doer of all of his actions, of course his beloved ego was the instigator of all such beliefs.

*M*ans ego is hidden so deeply in his psyche
and enabled by so many others in his life,
why indeed would he want to change or give
it up.

*T*he games of ones ego are best played upon
the playground of human unconsciousness.

*T*he destructive nature of mans ego must be reconciled with his divine higher self for any positive evolution to occur in his soul.

*T*he self created prison cell of the ego can only be opened with radical humility.

*T*he insecure human ego many times puts the happiness of others before its own.

*O*ur ego has us involved in a constant game of deception one that hides from us our true and higher self.

*T*he ego craves attention, favorable or not it doesn't matter.

⭐

*T*he illusory ego tries to convince us of its reality in the face of all contrary actions.

*T*here is always one major particular trait or habit of the ego that will keep the gates of the kingdom of heaven from being opened.

*T*he ego exists for the revelation that one day we will see it was the veil between us and our divine higher self.

*O*ur ego would rather have us withhold our love towards another rather than admit to any imaginary defeat.

★

*S*ome will ask "who am I "and the ego will answer while others will ask "who am I "and God will answer.

*A*t one time we will have to pay the price for the decisions that we have let our ego make for us.

*L*ife never seems more difficult than when it is lived exclusively through our ego.

*T*he ego perfumes man spirit with the stench of unhappiness.

★

*O*ur egos are the mechanism by which we as humans are able to learn the lessons necessary for the evolution of our spirit into divine oneness with our higher self.

*A*ll of life's drama has its genesis in the ego, for without the ego who would we be?

*H*umans have a silly and compulsive egoic need to try and convince another person that their way is the best or only way.

*O*ur ego inflates itself naturally in the course of events of ones life where we identify ourselves individually as the doer of those events.

*I*s there anything more hurtful to ones ego than the words of another?

*T*he ego masks from us our true identity and therefore has us operating at a severely diminished capacity.

✦

*O*ne mans egoic opinion has the weight and substance of a cloud passing overhead.

*M*any times we bend over backwards to protect and massage our sensitive and precious ego.

★

*T*he ego is rarely happy with "things as they are "therefore it creates the perception of the future for us to find our illusory happiness in.

*T*he ego is the ultimate skeptic for why should it embrace a new idea or way of thinking that might possibly lead to its demise?

*M*ans egoistic personality, the cause of many of his sufferings, has hypnotized him into believing that others are the cause of his unhappiness.

*T*he picture of life as painted by the ego is a false one as it is rooted in an illusion.

★

*W*hat you are is what you have always been.

*O*ur ego will one day disappear into the one universal consciousness and find its true home there.

*M*an has made his ego the captain of his ship and now must take back the helm for his own health and well being.

*P*ure consciousness is what remains after the individual ego has been annihilated.

*T*he common man is both baffled and confused by his ego.

*N*o time is more perfect than this instant to roll the dice and challenge ones ego with a dose of ones true higher and divine self.

★

*O*ur ego is a necessary phantom for us to be able to engage in everyday life.

The loudest voice that one should ever hear should be that of his intuition crying out over the din of the ego.

★

The ego likes to convince itself and others as to its expertise in may areas, so long as those areas don't include the ego.

A well modulated ego is not only a great gift to ones self but a great gift to humanity.

*T*he personal "I" disappears when we are aware of and contemplate our divine higher self.

*W*hat better way for us to cover up our imaginary insecurities than with the facade of the illusory ego.

*T*rue genius comes from the profound realization that we are not what our ego tells us that we are.

*D*esire generated by the ego and manifested in the personality further serves to create separation from both ourselves and others.

*W*e seem to think that the world and other people exist only for our benefit or better yet the benefit of our ego.

*T*he ego creates desires that are impossible to fulfill, but that is it's magic, for our constant striving means the ego will always have a necessary place in our lives.

★

*O*ur ego doesn't necessarily fear its demise as much as we do as humans fear losing the only thing that we know about ourselves to be true and real.

*T*he ego is an expert in all spiritual matters both great and small including those of spiritual pride.

★

*T*he momentary struggles of the human ego fade away and disappear with a conscious recognition of ones higher self.

*I*t would probably be a good idea to question all matters that have been generated by and approved for action by the ego.

A downsized ego removes from man his greatest impediment to success.

*T*he destiny that our ego has chosen for us is usually very different than the one that in actuality was our divine inheritance.

★

*T*o challenge ones ego to the fullest requires not only courage but large amounts of patience.

*T*he spiritual deficit caused by our ego is immeasurable.

*T*he ego is as passionate about its opinions as it is about proving another's opinions as being wrong.

*H*ow can we ever ask or expect another to give up their ego when it is all that they have ever known.

*O*nce the go has discovered a weakness it must be overcome or it can lead to ones destruction.

*T*he external happiness that humans seek is as much an illusion as the ego that leads them out on that path in the first place.

*M*any men live only to please their ego and in the end make no one happy.

*M*ans ego, more than his destiny takes what little free will that he has and imprisons it through his unconsciousness.

*T*he punishment that many are willing to endure to prolong the life of the ego is often quite radical indeed.

*O*ur current materialistic culture contributes to and inflates both the collective and individual ego with its narcissistic tendencies and outlook on life.

*W*e can grow and evolve more rapidly by doing those things that the ego doesn't want us to do.

*T*he best way to strengthen ones faith is through the weakening of the ego.

*T*he ego very rarely feels good and unequivocabally happy for the good fortune and success of another person unless it meets the conditions set forth by ones ego.

*T*he immature or unripened ego is the mechanism by which we are metaphysically disconnected from our true and higher self.

★

*T*he immature person is a victim of their underdeveloped ego.

The ego is that thing that makes it hard for us to get along with other people.

⭐

The ego carries with it a sense of entitlement, albeit a false one.

*A*n addiction is the ego's way of keeping our lower self in charge and hiding from us the potential of the divine higher self.

*M*ans ego plays the role of cosmic gatekeeper much to the chagrin of the higher self.

*H*ow can one even begin to understand the ego if they don't even know that they have one?

⭐

*M*ans mistaken belief that his ego is his true self and that it has unlimited power over him keeps him firmly entrenched in its bondage.

*T*he simplest way of living is not the most favorite way of the ego.

★

*M*ans selfish desires have inflated his ego beyond belief and created situations for him that are untenable.

*T*he ego hides its contempt for others under the guise of helpfulness and friendliness.

★

*T*he temper tantrum of the adult can be directly related to the unripened ego of the child.

*U*nbridled passions are the fuel of the foolish ego.

*T*he egos favorite subject is itself.

*T*he best way to describe the inflated ego would be unconsciousness unawareness.

★

*T*he games that people play both with themselves and others can be directly traced back to an unawareness of the power of their ego.

*T*here is only one truth but with the ego blocking our view there seems to be many.

✦

*T*he vulgar nature of ones ego requires that it be made the center of attention.

*T*he ego has us both entranced and befuddled with its illusory power.

*T*he ego makes us see the illusion of two when in fact there is only unicity.

*W*e must radically deconstruct the ego if we are to have any possible hope of freedom from it.

*T*he ego leads us into temptation to perpetuate its desire for drama and conflict in its world.

*H*uman beings intentions are almost always clouded by the expectations of their ego.

★

*T*he ego goes out of its way to prove its validity to others, but how futile is it to prove that which is an illusion just to sustain ones existence?

*T*rue change is impossible without a correct
awareness of ones ego.

*T*he ego does not only seek attention, it
demands attention.

*H*uman relations have become extremely shallow and false due to the materialistic nature of the human ego.

*T*he ego creates an illusion of pseudo power to further hypnotize one to its reality.

Communion with God is an egoless state of oneness that is eternal.

★

The ego is a lot less necessary than one would be lead to believe.

*M*ans greatest vanity is also his greatest stumbling block to freedom, it is called the ego.

*I*ndividual temptation is nothing more than the ego giving us a chance to justify our weaknesses.

*T*he ego favorite's subject is the ego, it loves nothing better to draw attention to and talk about itself.

★

*T*rue and natural humility is one of the most prominent features of the thinned out ego.

*M*any people ask the question: Who would I be without my ego? The answer is much deeper than would be found in our normal and everyday consciousness.

*T*he more stubborn the ego, the more suffering must take place before the higher self can gain a foothold.

The ego takes us on a never ending search for that which we already have.

★

The ego energizes the traits in ourselves that we most want to have quietly under control.

*D*o we have the free will to control and direct our ego?

*I*f the ego is self created illusion based on the image that we have of ourselves, who created the image that we developed the ego from anyway?

The ego creates an imaginary world where we think and believe that other people are actually interested in our thoughts and opinions.

★

The collective egoistic personalities of mankind are in a kind of dysfunctional synchronicity.

*T*he ego is a necessity for survival; however a blind allegiance to it is not.

★

*T*he bad decisions made by the ego must one day be solved by that very same ego.

*O*ne consciousness can elevate but ones ego can only inflate.

★

*T*he mystical necessity of the ego is such that without it the evolution of the human species could not take place.

*W*e must create diversions for ourselves that don't include us blindly following the ego.

⭐

*T*he ego very cleverly hides from us our true and divine higher self.

The ego seems so real and plausible when we are under its spell.

***

The almighty ego has become for many people the shrine in which they worship.

*T*he ego has created for us a world of illusion
that can only be escaped from with a radical
dose of reality.

★

*T*o many humans the ego is as unknowable
as it is unconquerable.

*T*ime is an illusion created by the ego to keep from communion with our higher self.

*T*he dream of the ego dissolves under a radical awareness of our divine and higher self.

*T*he timeless state of the higher self is the enemy of the time bound ego.

★

*T*he ego has a very prominent place in the process of human evolution.

*O*ur current society has succeeded in supersizing just about everything including the ego.

⭐

*T*he ego is not prejudiced by the actions of others.

The ego is that insubstantial part of ourselves that we take to be our real self.

★

The ego masquerades as the truth when in fact it is a mere shadow of it.

*F*ear and desire are the fuel of the ego that contributes to both its power and its inflation.

★

*T*he ego creates a constant and many times a consistent state of unfulfilled desires.

The lessons taught by the ego are eternal.

The ego exists in time; the higher self exists in timelessness.

*T*he puzzles and riddles of life cannot be solved by the lower self.

*T*he ego isn't as much selfish as it is deceitful.

*T*he ego has a very radical desire to divide and conquer.

★

*I*f ones ego is such that it doesn't need the praise of others, then freedom is a distinct possibility.

*W*e feed our minds with junk food and we wonder why our souls are malnourished.

*T*he individual ego seeks to prove its necessity in every moment and in every conceivable way.

*W*e must go to the very point where all conceptualization begins to become aware of and begin to thin out the insidious methods of the ego.

*H*ow can we trust our egoistic personality when it is simply the image that we have of ourselves as seen by others.

*T*he "I AM" before conceptualization takes place is devoid of the ego.

*T*imelessness is a state of consciousness away from and separate from the egoistic mind.

*T*he life blood of the ego is conceptualization for without it the ego will die.

★

*T*he ego creates the unsatisfactory environment from which we try to seek satisfactory results.

*T*he delusion that we are a small and separate ego in this vast and complex universe can only lead one to the question "what or who am I "

*S*elf pride is a faculty of the ego that gives us a false sense of personal doer ship and thus inflates the ego to sometimes epic proportions.

*A*ll of the elements necessary to perpetuate the drama of human living are contained in the ego.

★

*T*he human ego seeks to find permanence in an otherwise impermanent world.

*E*go inflation is the human response to fear.

*T*he perfect consequences of cause and effect are expressed through man's ego.

*T*he ego points us in many directions most usually to the path of least resistance.

★

*T*he ego gives man an excuse to be irresponsible and unaware of his higher self.

The death of the ego seems like a far away concept; however its demise can start at this very moment.

The ego is the most necessary element for the play of life to continue.

*A*ll dualism is caused by the ego to keep the human organism hypnotized into the illusion of separateness.

★

*T*he ego seeks to assert its superiority through our weakness' and not our strengths.

*W*hen the ego dies we then have the freedom to live.

*T*he truth of life hidden by the ego can only be uncovered by a radical awareness of the very same ego.

*T*he human being in many cases is unaware of their higher self and therefore must suffer needlessly at the hands of the lower self or ego.

★

*M*ans egoistic personality at some point becomes a point of personal pride which must be defended at any cost.

*T*he trials and tribulations of the individual ego are quite fascinating indeed.

*T*he ego picks chooses those things upon which it will deceive us.

*T*he ego is never one to consider the consequences of its actions.

★

*M*an's passion and ardor for his ego is unsurpassed.

*T*he ego's ability is greatly overrated.

*T*he transgressions of the ego are the self created problems of the unaware lower self.

*T*he blind allegiance to the ego takes place only because of a lack of faith and knowledge of ones divine and higher self.

*T*he reward for a person of high virtue is a clear conscience.

*T*he dualistic nature of man's ego is both the source and creation of his bondage.

*T*he ego leads us to believe that there are many versions of the truth when in fact there is just one.

*M*ans sense of personal doer ship is the egos way of hypnotizing us into the belief that we cannot survive without it.

*T*he mechanisms used by the ego to maintain its existence are surprisingly sophisticated.

*I*n life's journeys many times we have made
the ego our tour guide.

★

*A*ll doubts come from the ego, in ones higher
self there are known.

*T*he world is a lot less interested in you than your ego would like you to believe.

★

*W*hen we take things personally it is the ego way of telling us that we are a sole and separate entity in the Universe.

*T*he surrendering of the ego is better known as the divine awakening.

★

*T*he desires of the ego keep us from seeing the freedom of the higher self.

*T*he kingdom of heaven awaits those for whom the burden of the ego has become to great.

*O*nes ego is many times a reflection of a person's inner self.

*M*ans ego is an incomplete replica of his higher self.

★

*W*hen seen from totality the ego is a false purveyor of truth.

*U*nbridled passion fuels and inflates the ego through the illusion of the senses.

*T*he ego tortures us with memories of the past and anxiety about the future.

*T*he individual consciousness of the ego is a weak imposter for the powerful spirit of the higher self.

★

*T*he bondage of the ego is a mere reflection or shadow of our higher self.

*M*any times the ego is not only our best friend but our only friend.

✦

*T*he ego demands that we pay it attention, so in a sense we could say that the ego is the high maintenance part of our personalities.

*E*very blind alley that the ego leads us down is one less experience that we need to suffer through again.

*A*ll of the weakness' that have in ourselves are the first things that we notice in others.

*A*fter all material avenues have been explored the human organism will then naturally turn towards the spiritual.

⭐

*L*et compassion be your greatest virtue.

*T*he egocentric self is always at odds with the higher self.

*T*he drama of life could not continue and flourish without the beloved ego.

*T*he ego keeps us engaged in the pursuit of the superficial until such time as we evolve into the spirit of our higher self.

★

*T*he ego is made possible through the process of divine hypnosis.

*T*he most important thing that we can ask ourself is: How can anything be different than it really is? No matter what the ego would lead us to believe.

*T*he ego feels free to judge others but in itself feels unworthy of judgment.

*T*he struggle with ones higher self must be solved with a compromise with ones ego.

★

*T*he ego keeps man locked in a prison of space and time from which the only escape is an apperception of the totality of all existence.

*A*ll unhappiness and suffering originates in the conceptual thinking of the egoic personality.

The ego serves as a compass to point us in the direction that we need to go in for our maximum growth and evolution.

*A*ll desire is preceded by a concept which was caused by a thought.

★

*T*he universal consciousness leaves it up to the individual whether to accept or reject any thoughts.

*I*n the complete and total surrender of the ego one finds the joy and miracle of the Cosmos.

*A*n ego trip is not a vacation.

A life lived in obedience to ones ego is devoid of hope and impartial to evolution.

W hat or who would we are without the ego? For many humans that question is unanswerable.

We can always count on the ego to tell us that things are great even in the face of all contrary information.

★

When we make the ego the sole captain of our ship we are no longer in charge of our destiny.

*T*he ego is the incomplete or distilled version of our higher self that we mistakenly take on as our true entity.

★

*O*ne must be in great suffering or inner turmoil to want to challenge the authority of ones ego.

*T*he ego only exists in the awakened state, for without awakened consciousness would it even exists?

*M*any times we neglect the love of those closest to us for the illusory love of ones ego.

*I*f the only lesson that we take from this life is to become radically aware of our illusory ego then we have had a successful lifetime.

*T*he ego is the immature byproduct of a dysfunctional environment.

*W*ithout a sense of separateness the ego would have no existence.

★

*T*he ego is not something to mad at or afraid of, just something to be AWARE of.

*T*rue freedom is available here and now, but
only through the surrender of the beloved
ego.

★

*T*hrough identification with his ego man
chooses to suffer, through identification with
his higher self man chooses happiness and
freedom

By not doing anything; some people do quite a bit.

★

Shame is the by product of all ego generated and initiated actions.

*T*he more gigantic the ego; the larger and more destructive it's potential misfortunes.

*W*e say to other how great our lives are; but is that just the ego talking?

*U*nicity being our true state solves the problems created the dual nature of the ego.

★

*T*he ego has sold many an illusory bill of goods called duality.

*A*t the moment of its annihilation, the ego will merge into the impersonal

★

*U*niversal coconsciousness and what remains is the pure animating consciousness of the Universe in that human organism.

*T*he addictive nature of jealousy, envy and gossip lend themselves very nicely to the insecure aspects of the human ego

★

*H*ow can we fault the ego for becoming captain of our ship, when in fact we were unaware of any other alternatives?

*T*he satisfactions of the ego are very short lived.

★

*W*hen one sees the hollowness of the egos pleasures, the search for something deeper and more fulfilling takes over.

*T*he ego creates problems that seem on the surface to be of the "life and death" variety but upon closer and deeper inspection are no more real than the dreams one has when sleeping.

★

*T*he sometimes hellish struggle with the ego can only be transcended by a direct apperception of the unity of all of existence.

Without the ego how would God keep the game of life going?

★

Selfishness and greed are the two primary sources that the ego uses to keep the human being hypnotized.

*N*o information in the universe is "new" only the interpretation of it is.

★

*M*ans biggest folly is not in his mindless loyalty to his ego but in not considering that that there might be another alternative.

*E*verything that we do to deny love in either ourselves or in the world inflates the ego.

★

*F*or the love of his ego man not only suffers but tortures himself needlessly.

*T*he illusory separation between out lower self, the ego and our higher self is nothing more than a by product of our false imagination.

*T*rue selfishness is the thought that we are only the ego and act as such in total denial and ignorance of our higher self.

*T*he illusory separation between out lower self, the ego and our higher self is nothing more than a by product of our false imagination.

*T*rue selfishness is the thought that we are only the ego and act as such in total denial and ignorance of our higher self.

*T*he ego has many people living life while looking through the rearview mirror.

*M*ost people that are looking out for their own good have no idea what their own good is.

*M*ans transparent "self help" is simply ego knowledge only and does not include any knowledge of ones higher self.

*A*s we become more dispassionate about our ego we find that we need and use it less and less to make our decisions for us.

*T*he ego is only motivated by being on what it thinks is the path of least resistance.

*W*hat we think we want and what makes our life easy only serves to strengthen the ego.

*T*o ignore the ego is the best way to transcend it.

*T*he ego tries many times to convince us many times to our detriment that true happiness is available to us in the sensorially perceived material world only.

*W*ho would we be without our ego?

*A*t the very moment that you think that you finally understand your ego, you must realize that you don't.

*J*ust when you think that you have surrendered your ego fully you will find out that you haven't.

*A*ll the things that we do to deny love in ourselves or in the world simply inflates the ego.

*B*eautiful thoughts usually lead to beautiful actions.

*T*he ego thrives on the illusory sense of separation between ourselves and God.

*T*he true Sage knows that by knowing nothing he in fact knows everything.

*T*he egos main purpose is to create a purpose for you in life so as to maintain the illusion that life has a purpose.

*T*he ego is full of surprises, the longer we live the more of them that we will see.

★

*T*he ego has us convinced that our problems are real!

The ego creates an eternal veil of separation until, according to Nature one is awakened from the dream of life and true understanding takes place.

★

The egos happiness is short lived as it finds its happiness in the transitory material word.

*O*ur ego tells us who we are and we believe it every time!

✯

*M*an's greatest challenge is to go to the core of his ego and expose it for the illusion that it is.

*T*he ego is the great lover of mischief and nonsense.

★

*E*goistic desires begin and end in human suffering.

*T*he ego usually doesn't know right from wrong it only knows its desires.

★

*I*s there anything of less value than ones out of control ego?

*T*he same amount of God exists in everyone;
it is only the ego that tells us that it isn't so.

★

*T*he ego subconsciously courts conflict in
order to prove its superiority.

*T*he Egos greatest wish is have all of its desires met without resistance.

★

*C*onsciousness in most humans is primarily a game of anticipation.

*T*here is nothing to know and no one to know it.

⭐

*T*he ego through divine hypnosis has created an individual with a name and a past and future through which universal perfection can take place.

One might be able to say when viewing their problems that their ego may have gotten the best of them.

✪

Mans greatest courage is needed in the surrender of his ego.

*B*y not doing anything quite a bit can get done.

★

*U*nicity being our true state solves the problems cause by the duality of the ego.

*E*goistic desires run wild when not balanced with awareness.

★

*M*ans dual nature is necessary for the game of life to continue as it does.

No one has ever won an argument with God.

⭐

Mans divine nature lies hidden behind the illusion of his ego.

*W*e could become very good friends with our ego if we just didn't let it run the show to the exclusion of our happiness and well being.

⭐

*I*f we are able to pacify our ego then we can begin to purify our soul.

*W*ho we think we are disappears into
Unicity when we have completely
surrendered our ego to the universal self.

*T*he courage to be who you truly are requires
copious amounts of faith and patience.

*I*n all persons lies a desire for happiness, in few persons is that desire directed in a positive manner.

*T*he misdirected ego finds illusory happiness in another's pain.

When all is said and done what has actually been said and what was actually done?

★

The sense of personal doership has created the illusion of suffering from which we seek escape.

*O*ur true salvation comes from the surrender of the ego to the higher self.

★

*W*e are most commonly disrespected by our ego, yet we most usually want to blame others.

*T*he transformation from the ego driven self to the oneness of universal consciousness is proof that miracles do occur.

*W*hen we leave behind that which we found to be hollow, we then are free to experience true freedom as the whole self.

*B*ondage is created by desires that the ego tells us that we must fulfill to be happy.

★

*I*n most humans, happiness is a transitory state caused by our reliance on an illusory self called the ego for its sustenance.

*T*he complete deconstruction of the false self called the ego is necessary for us to be able to enter the kingdom of heaven.

★

*G*enerosity of spirit comes to full fruition with the apperception that no separate "me" ever truly existed.

*M*ans emotions and desires are simply movements in the universal consciousness.

★

*T*he egoistic desires of man will require greater amounts of stimulation if they not seen for the illusion that they are.

*W*e become desensitized to the ego and soon
follow it unquestionly to one unhappy
situation after another never once seeking the
source of our suffering.

⭐

*B*y seeing the true source of our being we are
able to transcend desire and purify ourselves
in the spirit.

*T*he ego takes a thought and personalizes it just so that we consider it our own and thereby be subject to the whims of the ego.

*A*ll of life is impersonal; it is our conceptualization of it that makes it personal.

*T*he ego takes up a lot of time trying to convince us of all the things that we cannot do.

★

*F*reedom from the illusion of ego can only happen when one sees that there wasn't anyone that needed freedom to begin with.

Most humans consider their ego to be a very viable part of their lives and would consider it an affront to be told that the very same ego that is held in such regard is the constant cause of all of their unhappiness.

Mans egoic nature breeds a certain kind of false living where the false is seen as true and vice versa.

*T*rue bondage is when one becomes a slave to the desires of ones ego.

*F*alse imagination is the creator of all of life's hardships.

*A*ll happiness that is derived from the ego and its wants and desires will be hollow and short lived.

*All imagined attempts at volition are exposed as illusory and false when seen from Unicity.

*T*he One appears as many when seen through the eyes of the ego.

★

*T*he ego creates a sense of personal ownership and doership, but in the end who owns or does what?

*T*he ego creates the characters in the play called life.

*A*ll of life is divine even our egoic desires.

*L*ife's greatest desires would not be possible
without the human ego.

*T*he egos greatest problem is in seeing the all
of differences between humans rather than
their oneness.

*T*he ego creates many from the One and
fear, pain and desire are the direct result.

*L*ife's greatest mysteries are solved when all
of the various me's are seen as the one "I".

*D*uplicity creates all of the illusory problems which then must be solved by the illusory ego.

★

*L*ife is one continuous and never-ending process through which humans are the process by which the necessary events of cosmic evolution can occur.

*W*hat we think about ourselves are the images that we have constructed over the years with the help of our ego to form that person who we think that we are.

★

*P*ersonal volition is never a factor in any of the events that make up the course of human history.

*T*he less that we depend on our ego for happiness the greater our happiness will be.

★

*D*esire is a false thought created by an illusory need for fulfillment in a future that does not exist.

*F*ear comes from desire, a desire for things to be the way that we want them to be.

★

*S*ecurity of any kind is an illusion in this Universe of Gods creation not mans.

*M*ankind is frustrated because it seeks to understand life from a human perspective when our lives have been determined and created from a source that is most admittedly not human or understandable by the egoic humans mind.

*O*ur negative desires cannot be controlled but they can be ignored.

*T*he human ego has in essence created all of mans suffering through its false imagination and illusory sense of personal doership.

★

*I*f man was aware of his true nature instead of hypnotically attracted to that which is false all of life's questions would instantly be answered.

*O*ur opinions are the egos way of telling us that we know something better or differently than everyone else.

★

*W*ithout the ego who would we be or better yet how would be able to relate to others and the world?

*H*ow ironic that in our times of most desperate need we turn to the illusory ego for the solution.

⭐

*H*ow joyful and exuberant to be free of the bondage of ego and at one with our true and higher self!

*T*he ego loves to play the role of the great trickster, telling us things about ourselves that are far from true and then having us believe them.

★

*T*hat which man truly seeks relief from is himself or better yet his ego.

*M*an sometimes seeks relief from his suffering through the belief that he himself is not the cause of it that is his ego speaking to him.

*T*he first step in the annihilation of the ego is admitting to ones self that all of our problems were the result of the "me" and not from anyone else.

*T*he Universe will only give up as many secrets as you are willing to discover.

*M*any times it is much easier to see things not as they are but as we are.

When we rediscover our true and higher self we see that it was who and what we really were all along.

★

The ego wants to involve itself in all of our matters; in that respect you could call the ego a "busybody!"

The Sage has no "me" to satisfy or protect.

The transformation from the "me" to the "I" can only come about when the "me" is exposed for the illusion that it is.

*T*he concept that we have of ourselves that holds all of our power is commonly called the Ego.

*A*ll energy spent feeding the ego can only lead to the starvation of the soul.

*M*ost of us carry around two people everyday, our true and higher self and the image that we have of ourselves commonly known as the ego.

*W*hat more is the ego in the end than a simple concept albeit a mighty one?

*M*ans struggles are the by product of his false imagination which has its genesis in the ego.

*O*ur minds and thoughts are like magnets, they attract to us exactly what we put out.

*T*he crown jewel of life is "peace of mind" which can only come about as a result of seeing the illusion of the ego.

★

*H*uman beings are concepts that give themselves reality through the belief that their ego is real.

*T*he ego is like a mirage the closer that we get to it the farther away it seems to go.

★

*E*goic attachment to material pleasures cause pain and suffering when those same material pleasures are not available anymore.

*T*he dualistic viewpoint of living will cease to exist when the eternal moment of now is allowed to be.

★

*A*ll action has its genesis in the "I" when we take our actions to be from the "me" we have falsely chosen to limit ourselves to the ego.

*O*ne of life's biggest dichotomies is that the annihilation of the ego takes place on a path with no particular end to it.

★

*A*ll sense based experiences are the result of unfulfilled egoistic desires.

*P*atience and faith are the two most necessary ingredients in the discovery of ones true nature.

★

*W*e can never truly hide from the ego, it can and will reveal itself at any moment and usually at the most inopportune time.

*A*ll humans are not the same; however they are the same consciousness.

★

*T*he egos tenacity must never be underestimated, as it has an almost subhuman survival instinct.

You don't have to do every thing that the ego tells you that you must do.

★

Ones true self is mere shadow compared to what the ego wants you to believe about yourself.

*O*ne's image is a byproduct of and the meaning of the illusory ego.

★

A persons ego tells them that they must suffer, so they seek out situations in which suffering will occur.

*I*n ones true state suffering is never an option.

★

*L*ove is the most powerful weapon in ones struggle with the ego.

*M*ans egoic nature has become his most prevalent nature.

✫

*W*hen one is ready to ask" who am I " the ego has a more limited space in which to operate.

*R*adical egoism is a thief of compassion and an enemy of kindness.

★

*O*ne must be who they are but one must also become what he will.

*T*houghts and conceptions are like steroids for the human ego.

★

*T*he ego would like you to believe that it is your friend and has your best interests at heart; therein lies the dichotomy of the human ego.

*T*he ego is more duplicitous than we could ever imagine with our limited knowledge of its actions.

A humble nature is the perfect antidote for an out of control ego.

*O*ur ego is the first thing that tells us who we are when we begin to think about ourselves.

*A*lthough it may seem like the ego is the most necessary part of ones personality, by nature of its illusory qualities it does not have to dictate our lives to us when in fact we are the eternal and indestructible source of all life now and forever.

www.ingramcontent.com/pod-product-compliance
Lightning Source LLC
Chambersburg PA
CBHW030920090426
42737CB00007B/265